LUCY LIU

Actress, Artist, and Activist

Therese Shea

Enslow Publishing
101 W. 23rd Street
Suite 240
New York, NY 10011
USA

enslow.com

Words to Know

activist—One who acts strongly in support of or against an issue.

ambassador—A person who travels to another country to represent a group.

auditioned—Tried out for a role.

confidence—The feeling that one can succeed.

exhibit—A show displaying one's artwork.

immigrant—A person who comes to live in a new country.

nominated—Suggested someone for an honor.

sequel—A movie that continues the story begun in a previous movie.

Contents

Words to Know 2

CHAPTER 1   Early Dreams 5

CHAPTER 2   The Road to Stardom............ 9

CHAPTER 3   Art and Activism 14

CHAPTER 4   Pushing Boundaries 19

Timeline........................... 22

Learn More 23

Index 24

Lucy Liu

CHAPTER 1

Early Dreams

Lucy Liu is a popular Chinese American actress as well as a successful artist. Lucy stands out for another reason: she uses her fame and talent to be an **activist** for women and children in need around the world.

Lucy was born on December 2, 1968, in New York City. Her parents, Cecilia and Tom, were Chinese **immigrants**. Because they only spoke Mandarin Chinese at home, Lucy did not learn to speak English until she was five years old. She graduated from the well-known Stuyvesant High School in New York in

1986 and then began at New York University. After one year, Lucy decided to attend the University of Michigan in Ann Arbor, where she focused on Asian studies.

Lucy's First Role

Besides Asian studies, Lucy also took college classes in dance, voice, fine arts, and acting. During her

Lucy Liu, pictured here in her high school yearbook, wanted to act from an early age. However, she had doubts since she did not see many Asian actors.

Lucy attended the University of Michigan, where she started to become serious about acting.

senior year, she tried out for a small part in the school's production of *Alice in Wonderland*. She won the lead role instead.

Lucy Says:

"[By winning the role in *Alice in Wonderland*] I realized you can be anything you want in the world. You don't have to follow what's given."

Lucy was surprised. The part of Alice is usually played by someone with blonde hair and blue eyes. The role gave her the **confidence** to pursue acting. She graduated from the university in 1990 and decided to move to Los Angeles, California, to begin her acting career.

CHAPTER 2

The Road to Stardom

Lucy did not become a star right away. She had many small parts at first. Her first television role was on *Beverly Hills, 90210* in 1991. She took little parts on several other shows, too. Her first movie appearance was in *Jerry Maguire*, a popular 1996 film.

Lucy's big break came when she **auditioned** for the television series *Ally McBeal*. She did not get the role she wanted, but the creator of the show, David E. Kelley, was impressed. He decided to make a part just for her. She was on the show from 1998 to 2001

Lucy's first major role was on *Ally McBeal*. She played a tough lawyer named Ling Woo.

and was **nominated** for an Emmy Award for Best Supporting Actress.

On the Big Screen

Lucy's television career helped her get noticed in the film business. She had roles in several movies, including starring as Princess Pei Pei in the hit comedy *Shanghai Noon* in 2000.

That same year, she appeared in *Charlie's Angels*. The movie was a remake of a television show that had starred three white women. Lucy got the part even though she was Asian. Again, she broke through a race barrier, just as she had in *Alice in Wonderland*. The movie was a huge hit, and Lucy appeared in its **sequel**, *Charlie's Angels: Full Throttle*, in 2003.

Lucy stands with her *Charlie's Angels* costars, Drew Barrymore (left) and Cameron Diaz.

Lucy also had a major role in the movies *Kill Bill: Vol. 1* (2003) and *Kill Bill: Vol. 2* (2004). She starred as a feared gang leader.

Breaking More Barriers

In the 2000s, Lucy appeared on television shows such as *Ugly Betty*, *Cashmere Mafia*, and *Dirty Sexy Money*. In 2012, she joined the cast of *Southland*. For this series, she won a 2012 Critics' Choice Award for Best Guest Performer in a Drama Series.

Lucy Says:

"It's really taking a while but I do think it's becoming more acceptable to cast Asians in roles that weren't originally slated for someone who is Asian, which is so great."

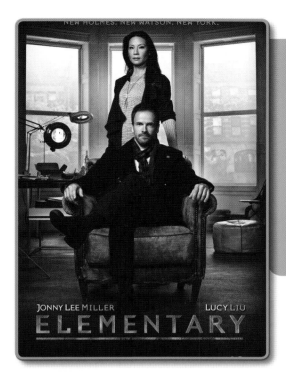

In 2012, Lucy was offered a surprising role in the television series *Elementary*, based on the Sherlock Holmes stories. She was asked to play Dr. Joan Watson, a woman helping Holmes solve crimes in today's New York City.

Some people were shocked that Dr. Watson was to be played by a woman. Lucy was happy to break another barrier. Audiences loved the show. Lucy has even directed several episodes.

CHAPTER 3

Art and Activism

Even while Lucy was trying out for roles in the 1990s, she still made time for her artwork. She began showing her paintings and photographs in galleries in New York. She used her Chinese name Yu Ling on her art. Many people did not know Yu Ling and Lucy Liu were the same person!

Lucy has had **exhibits** in Los Angeles, Miami, Munich, and London. She put out a book of artwork in 2013 called *Seventy Two*. In 2015, she released her artwork online on the website lucyliu.net.

Lucy stands in front of two pieces of her artwork at a 2006 exhibit in New York City.

Making a Difference

Since 2004, Lucy has been an **ambassador** for UNICEF (United Nations Children's Fund). She has worked hard to help needy women and children worldwide, including a trip to the Democratic Republic of Congo to work with children who were forced to be soldiers.

Lucy has also traveled to Peru, Russia, Pakistan, Egypt, Côte d'Ivoire, and Lesotho to visit with

Lucy Says:

"[UNICEF] is something I intend to be involved in for the rest of my life. Up until the moment I have my last breath, I am hoping there will be a way to create change."

Lucy says that being an ambassador for UNICEF has altered her life forever.

people in need of clean water, food, education, and health care. She hopes her fame will bring attention and aid for these people.

Aid Through Art

Lucy's passions for art and helping people have come together in her UNICEF work. She has held exhibits to raise money for the organization. She has used her talent as a photographer to capture

Lucy receives the World Social Award for her positive influence on the world. Standing next to her is former Prime Minister of Pakistan Benazir Bhutto.

important moments in her travels. She also donated a portion of the profits from her book *Seventy Two* to UNICEF.

In 2009, Lucy produced a film called *Redlight* about women and children sold into slavery. She also directed the award-winning short film *Meena*, the true story of a woman who escaped from slavery. For her ongoing work, Lucy was given the Champion of Peace Award from the Women for Women International in 2012.

CHAPTER 4
Pushing Boundaries

Lucy Liu continues to push boundaries and break barriers in her life and work. She has performed on Broadway in the Tony Award–winning play *God of Carnage*. She has done voice work in animated films such as *Kung Fu Panda* and on TV shows such as *The Simpsons*. She looks forward to doing more work behind the camera as a director, too.

Lucy is known for playing strong, talented women. Her **UNICEF** efforts and artwork are proof she is a woman of strength and talent in real life.

When Lucy was young, she did not think she could be an actress since she did not see actors who looked like her. Today, she is inspiring others to pursue their dreams, no matter their race or background.

Lucy Says:

"I strive to not deny myself experiences that open up to me. I hope to live without looking back in regret. If people want to join me on the ride, then I'm happy to have them along."

Timeline

1968—Lucy is born on December 2 in New York City.

1990—Graduates from University of Michigan with a degree in Asian studies.

1991—Appears on the television show *Beverly Hills, 90210*.

1998—Begins her role on *Ally McBeal*.

2000—Appears in *Shanghai Noon* and *Charlie's Angels*.

2004—Becomes an ambassador for UNICEF.

2008—Wins the Danny Kaye Humanitarian Award for her UNICEF work.

2012—Begins her role as Dr. Joan Watson in *Elementary*.

2012—Wins the Champion of Peace Award from Women for Women International.

2013—Puts out the art book *Seventy Two*.

2015—Releases her artwork online.

Learn More

Books

Kingston, Anna. *Respecting the Contributions of Asian Americans*. New York: PowerKids Press, 2012

Liu, Lucy. *Seventy Two*. London: Salma Editions, 2011.

Marsico, Katie. *UNICEF*. North Mankato, MN: Cherry Lake, 2014.

Onsgard, Bethany. *Asia*. Edina, MN: Core Library, 2013.

Websites

biography.com/people/lucy-liu-9542370#synopsis
Read a short biography of Lucy's life.

people.com/people/lucy_liu/biography/
Read a timeline of Lucy's rise to fame.

lucyliu.net
Find out more about Lucy's art on this official site.

Index

Alice in Wonderland, 7, 8, 11

Ally McBeal, 9

Asian Americans, 5, 11, 12

Broadway, 19

Champion of Peace Award, 18

Charlie's Angels, 11

Critics' Choice Award, 12

Elementary, 13

Emmy Award, 10

Kill Bill, 12

Meena, 18

New York University, 6

Redlight, 18

Seventy Two, 14, 18

Shanghai Noon, 10

Sherlock Holmes, 13

Stuyvesant High School, 5

UNICEF, 16, 17, 18

University of Michigan in Ann Arbor, 6

voice work, 19

Yu Ling, 14

Published in 2017 by Enslow Publishing, LLC.
101 W. 23rd Street, Suite 240, New York, NY 10011

Library of Congress Cataloging-in-Publication Data
Names: Shea, Therese, author.
Title: Lucy Liu : actress, artist, and activist / Therese Shea.
Description: New York : Enslow Publishing, [2017] | Series: Exceptional Asians | Includes bibliographical references and index.
Identifiers: LCCN 2015044483| ISBN 9780766078420 (library bound) | ISBN 9780766078482 (pbk.) | ISBN 9780766078109 (6-pack)
Subjects: LCSH: Liu, Lucy, 1968---Juvenile literature. | Actresses--United States--Biography--Juvenile literature.
Classification: LCC PN2287.L475 S54 2016 | DDC 791.4302/8092--dc23
LC record available at http://lccn.loc.gov/2015044483

Printed in Malaysia

To Our Readers: We have done our best to make sure all website addresses in this book were active and appropriate when we went to press. However, the author and the publisher have no control over and assume no liability for the material available on those websites or on any websites they may link to. Any comments or suggestions can be sent by e-mail to customerservice@enslow.com.

Photo Credits: Throughout book, ©Toria/Shutterstock.com (blue background); cover, p. 1 Debby Wong/Shutterstock.com; p. 4 Paul Morigi/WireImage/Getty Images; p. 6 Seth Poppel Yearbook Library; p. 7 Mark A. Johnson/Alamy Stock Photo; p. 10 Copyright © 20th Century Fox Film Corp./Everett Collection; p. 11 Kurt Vinion/Getty Images; p. 13 AF Archive/Alamy Stock Photo; p. 15 Scott Gries/Getty Images; p. 17 Karen Bleier/AFP/Getty Images; p. 18 Peter Kramer/Getty Images; p. 20 Stephen Lovekin/Getty Images.